AAT Professional Diploma in Accounting

Level 4

Business Tax

Finance Act 2020

Fifth edition 2020

ISBN 9781 5097 3408 5

British Library Cataloguing-in-Publication Data
A catalogue record for this book is available from the British Library

Published by

BPP Learning Media Ltd
BPP House, Aldine Place
142-144 Uxbridge Road
London W12 8AA

www.bpp.com/learningmedia

Printed in the United Kingdom

Your learning materials, published by BPP Learning Media Ltd, are printed on paper obtained from traceable, sustainable sources.

The contents of this book are intended as a guide and not professional advice. Although every effort has been made to ensure that the contents of this book are correct at the time of going to press, BPP Learning Media makes no warranty that the information in this book is accurate or complete and accepts no liability for any loss or damage suffered by any person acting or refraining from acting as a result of the material in this book.

Welcome to BPP Learning Media's AAT **Passcards for Business Tax.**

- They **save you time**. Important topics are summarised for you.
- They incorporate **diagrams** to kick start your memory.
- They follow the overall **structure** of the BPP Text, but BPP Learning Media's AAT **Passcards** are not just a condensed book. Each card has been separately designed for clear presentation. Topics are self contained and can be grasped visually.
- AAT **Passcards** are **just the right size** for pockets and bags where bought for studying on the move.
- AAT **Passcards focus on the assessment** you will be facing.
- AAT **Passcards focus on the essential points** that you need to know in the workplace, or when completing your assessment.

Run through the complete set of **Passcards** as often as you can during your final revision period. The day before the assessment, try to go through the **Passcards** again! You will then be well on your way to completing the assessment successfully.

Good luck!

For reference to the Bibliography of the AAT Business Tax Passcards please go to: www.bpp.com/learning-media/about/bibliographies

The BPP **Question Bank** contains activities and assessments that provide invaluable practice in the skills you need to complete this assessment successfully.

1: Tax framework

Topic List

- Tax law and guidance
- Methods of operating a business
- Types of income
- Total/net/taxable income
- Tax computation
- Tax avoidance/evasion
- Ethics

In Business Tax, *you need an awareness of the law and guidance relevant to tax. You are expected to have a broad knowledge of how to compute an individual's income tax liability. This will allow you to give the best advice on the utilisation of business losses. However, income tax computations will not be required in* Business Tax *as they are assessed in* Personal Tax.

Tax law

- Statute Law: Acts of Parliament
- Case Law

Detailed regulations in Statutory Instruments (SIs)

Does not have force of law

HMRC Guidance

- HMRC website
- Guidance helps interpret tax law
- Wide range of guidance published including:
  - Statements of practice
  - Working together publications

Business taxes

Sole traders

Partnerships

- Pay income tax on trading profits
- Pay capital gains tax on gains of business assets
- Pay class 2 and class 4 National Insurance

Companies

- Pay corporation tax on trading profits
- Pay corporation tax on gains on business assets
- Pay National Insurance (not on this syllabus)

An individual may receive various types of income:

- Income from their business (trading income)
- Employment income
- Bank and building society interest
- Property income
- Dividends

Income for a tax year is included in the income tax computation.

- A tax year runs from 6 April to 5 April
- 2020/21 – 6.4.20 to 5.4.21

All types of income added together is called total income.

Total income minus trade losses is called net income.

Net income minus the personal allowance is taxable income.

Personal allowance

(£12,500 in 2020/21)

The personal allowance is gradually withdrawn if net income > £100,000.

Tax computation

Pro forma for calculating taxable income

	Non-savings income
	£
Trading income	X
Employment income	X
Property income	X
Total income	X
Less: trade losses	(X)
Net income	X
Less: personal allowance	(X)
Taxable income	X

Income tax liability on taxable income

	£
Basic rate income @ 20%	X
Higher rate income @ 40%	X
Additional rate income @ 45%	X
Income tax liability	X

Tax evasion

- Illegal
- To deliberately mislead tax authorities to reduce tax liabilities
- May result in fines or imprisonment

Tax avoidance

- Currently legal
- To make use of loopholes in tax legislation to reduce tax liabilities

Tax planning

- To ensure use is made of all available tax reliefs in the manner intended to minimise tax liabilities

Five fundamental principles

- Integrity
- Objectivity
- Professional behaviour
- Confidentiality
- Professional competence and due care

2: Computing trading income

Topic List

- Badges of trade
- Allowable and disallowable expenditure
- Trading allowance

In this chapter we will look at the badges of trade and at the computation of taxable trading profits for both individuals and companies. Whether the business is incorporated or unincorporated the tax computation will start with the adjustment to profits.

You are extremely likely to see a task where you need to adjust the accounts profit for tax purposes in your assessment. The best way to become proficient at this is to practise as many adjustments as you can.

Badges of trade

- The subject matter
- The frequency of transactions
- The length of ownership
- Supplementary work and marketing
- A profit motive
- The way in which the asset sold was acquired
- The reasons for sale
- The existence of similar trading transactions or interests
- The source of finance

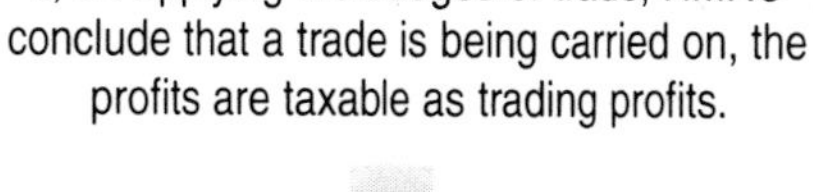

If, on applying the badges of trade, HMRC conclude that a trade is being carried on, the profits are taxable as trading profits.

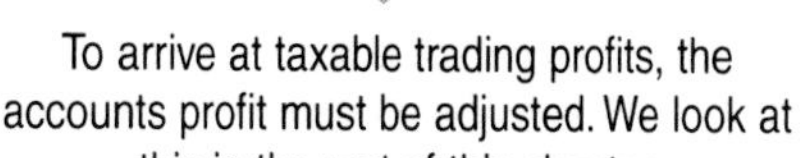

To arrive at taxable trading profits, the accounts profit must be adjusted. We look at this in the rest of this chapter.

Certain items of expenditure are not allowable for taxable trading profit purposes, and so must be added back to the accounts profit when computing such profits. Conversely other items are allowable.

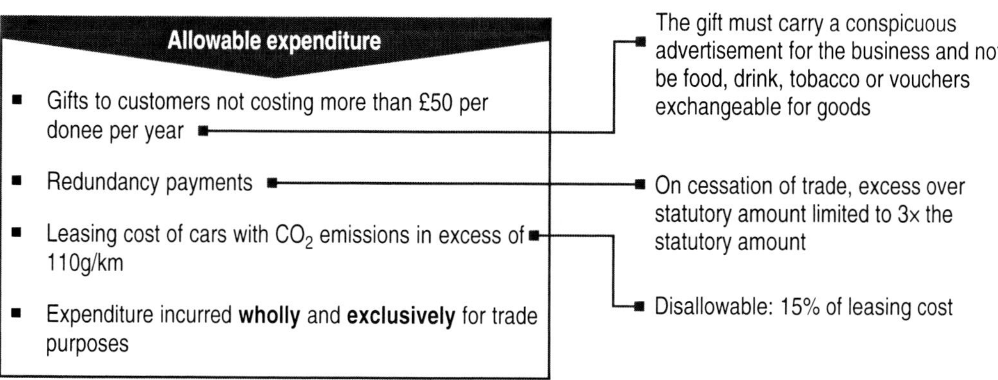

Disallowable expenditure

- Fines and penalties
  - Employee (not director) parking fines incurred whilst on employer's business are, however, allowed
- Depreciation, amortisation
- Salary/interest paid to sole trader/partner
- Private expenses of trader
  - Not applicable to a company
- Capital expenditure
  - The cost of initial repairs to make an asset fit to use is disallowable capital expenditure but the cost of initial repairs to remedy normal wear and tear is allowable
- Entertaining
  - Staff entertaining is allowed
- Legal fees relating to capital items
  - Fees relating to the renewal of a short lease are allowable
- General provisions
  - Disallow any general provision. A specific provision is however allowed
- Any expense not incurred **wholly** and **exclusively** for trade purposes
- Political donations
- Charitable donations unless small and local

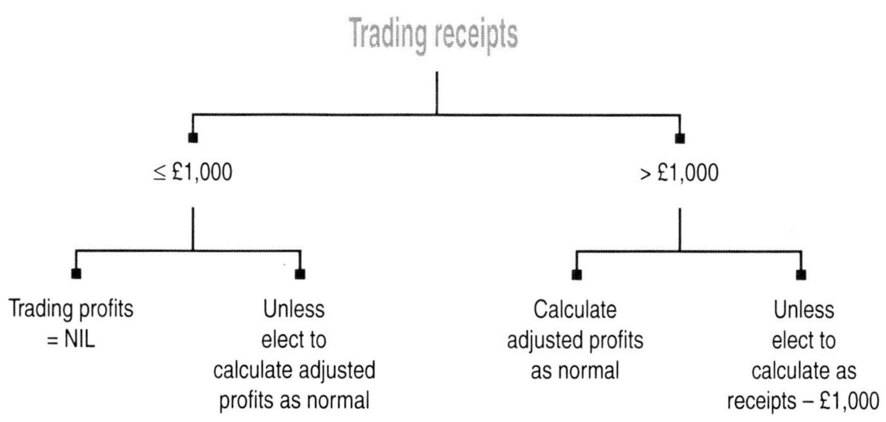
Trading receipts
≤ £1,000
> £1,000
Trading profits = NIL
Unless elect to calculate adjusted profits as normal
Calculate adjusted profits as normal
Unless elect to calculate as receipts – £1,000

Notes

3: Capital allowances

Topic List

Capital allowances are given instead of depreciation, but they are only available for certain classes of asset. They are a trading expense deducted in arriving at taxable trading profits.

Capital allowance computations

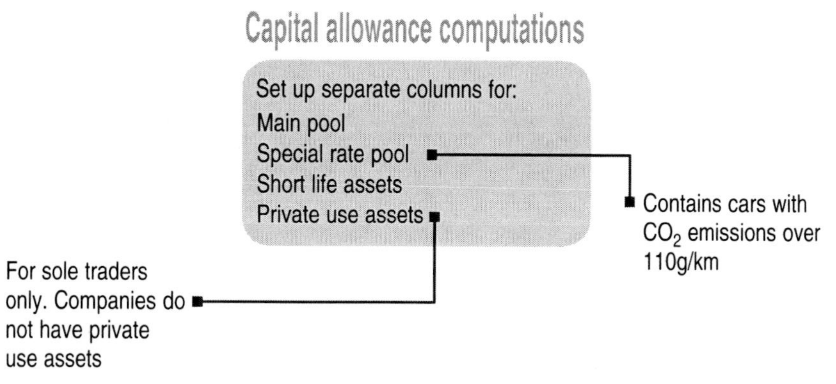

Annual investment allowance (AIA)

- Now £200,000 p.a. (£1,000,000 between 1.1.19 and 31.12.20)
- Scale up/down for short/long periods of account
- Use hybrid AIA for periods of account that straddle 1 January 2019 and 1 January 2021.

Writing down allowances (WDAs)

- 18% p.a. in main pool on a reducing balance basis
- 6% p.a. in special rate pool from 6.4.19 (8% before 6.4.19)
- Scale up/down × months/12 in short/long periods of account
- Reduced WDAs can be claimed
- Use hybrid rate if period of account straddles 6.4.19

Cars

- $CO_2 \leq$ 50g/km = 100% FYA
- CO_2 51g/km – 110g/km = main pool
- $CO_2 >$ 110g/km = special rate pool

100% First year allowance (FYA)

- Available on low emission cars and energy/water saving plant
  - Cars with CO_2 emissions $\leq$ 50g/km
- **Not** pro-rated in short/long periods

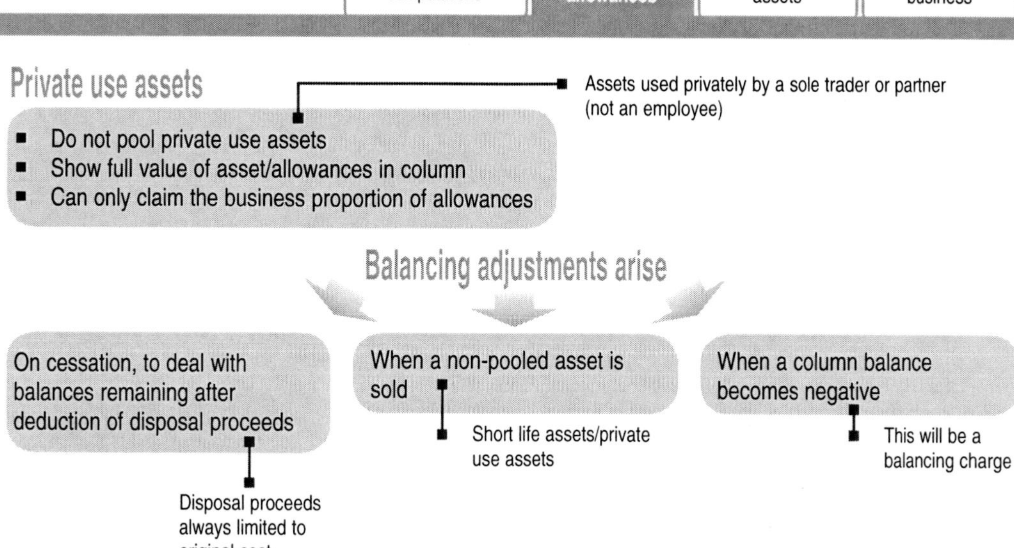
Private use assets
Assets used privately by a sole trader or partner (not an employee)
Do not pool private use assets
Show full value of asset/allowances in column
Can only claim the business proportion of allowances
Balancing adjustments arise
On cessation, to deal with balances remaining after deduction of disposal proceeds
Disposal proceeds always limited to original cost
When a non-pooled asset is sold
Short life assets/private use assets
When a column balance becomes negative
This will be a balancing charge

Short life assets (SLA)

- An election can be made to depool assets.
- Depooled assets must be disposed of within eight years of end of the period of acquisition.
- From a planning point of view depooling is useful if balancing allowances are expected.
- Conversely, in general, assets should not be depooled if they are likely to be sold within eight years for more than their tax written down values.

Not cars

Otherwise the balance of expenditure must be transferred back to main pool

This would result in a balancing charge

Cessation of business

In final period

- Add in any additions
- Deduct disposal proceeds (limited to cost)
- Assets kept by owner deemed to be sold at MV
- No FYA, AIA or WDA
- Give balancing adjustments to bring pools to zero

4: Computing corporation tax

Topic List

Taxable total profits

Accounting periods

Computing corporation tax payable

Companies pay corporation tax rather than income tax or capital gains tax (CGT).

In this chapter we will cover how taxable total profits are computed and the calculation of the corporation tax liability. This is likely to be an essential part of your assessment.

A company's taxable total profits are arrived at by aggregating its various sources of income and chargeable gains and then deducting qualifying charitable donations.

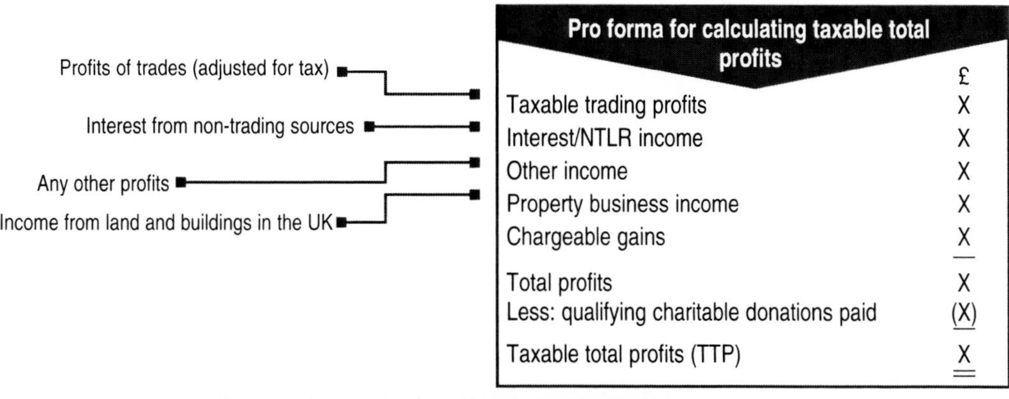

Pro forma for calculating taxable total profits

	£
Taxable trading profits	X
Interest/NTLR income	X
Other income	X
Property business income	X
Chargeable gains	X
Total profits	X
Less: qualifying charitable donations paid	(X)
Taxable total profits (TTP)	X

Dividends from other companies are not included in taxable total profits.

Interest/NTLR income

Interest income from non-trading sources minus interest payable on non-trading loans.

Examples of non-trading interest payable: loans to buy rental properties, or shares in a subsidiary

Property business income

All property business income is treated as a single source of income, calculated in the same way as trading profits.

You will not be expected to compute property business income in *Business Tax*, but you may be expected to include the income in arriving at taxable total profits

Companies must pay corporation tax on their **taxable total profits** in each **accounting period**.

An accounting period can never exceed 12 months. If a company prepares accounts for a period exceeding twelve months, this period of account must be split into two accounting periods.

The first 12 months form the first accounting period

The remaining months form the second accounting period

Example

If A Ltd prepares accounts for the fifteen months to 31.12.20, there will be one 12 month accounting period to 30.9.20 and a second 3 month accounting period to 31.12.20.

Long period of account

If a period of account exceeds 12 months, divide profits between the accounting periods as follows:

- Trading income: time apportion the amount before capital allowances
- Compute capital allowances separately for each period
- Interest income: allocate to the period in which it accrues
- Property business income and other income: time apportion
- Gains: allocate to the period in which they are realised
- Qualifying charitable donations: allocate to the period in which paid

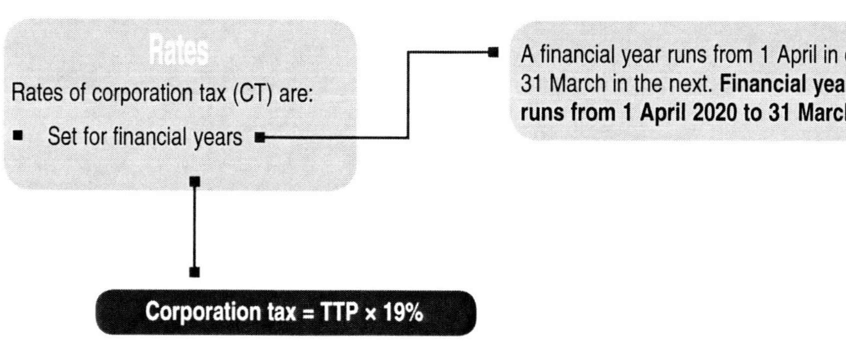
Rates
Rates of corporation tax (CT) are:
■ Set for financial years
A financial year runs from 1 April in one year to 31 March in the next. **Financial year 2020 (FY 2020) runs from 1 April 2020 to 31 March 2021.**
Corporation tax = TTP × 19%

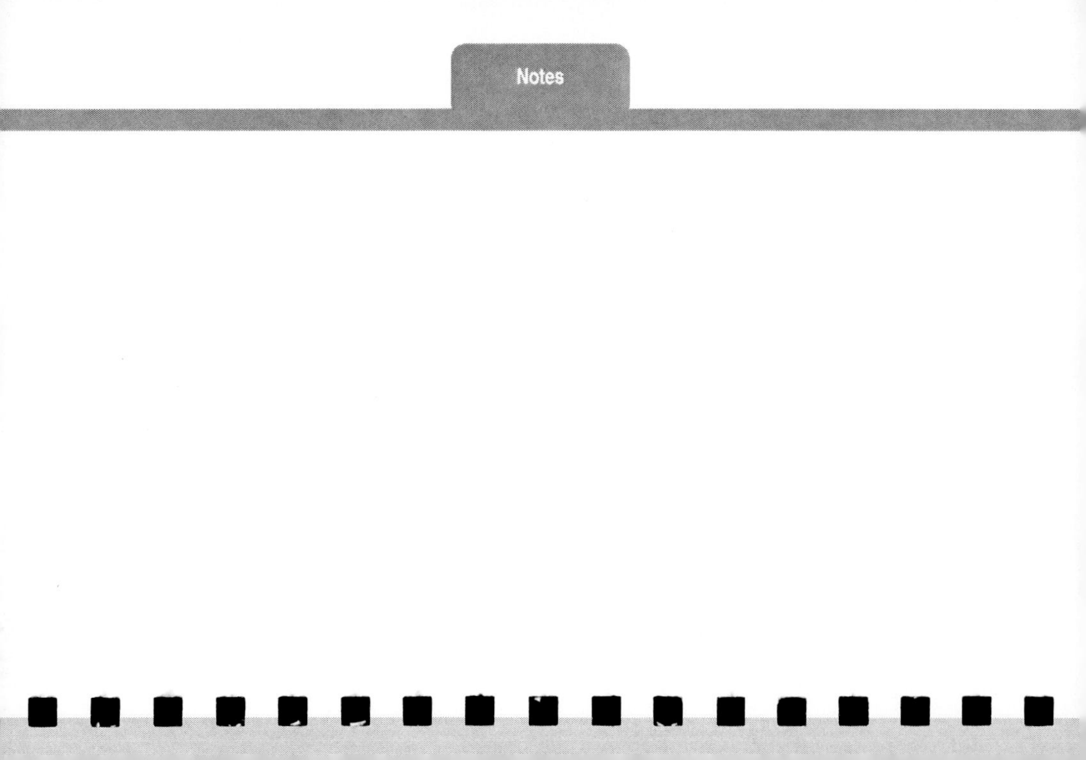

Notes

5: Taxing unincorporated businesses

Topic List

- Continuing business
- Opening years
- Overlap profits
- Final year
- Change of accounting date

The basis period rules are the rules whereby the profits of a period of account are linked to tax years.

These rules are vitally important for the purposes of the assessment and you must make sure you know them.

Remember these rules only apply to sole traders or partners in a partnership.

The basis period for each tax year is normally the period of account ending in that tax year.

Example

A sole trader makes up accounts to 31 December each year. The basis period for 2020/21 will be the year to 31 December 2020.

There are special basis period rules in opening and closing years.

Opening years

Year	1	2	3
Basis period	Date of commencement – 5 April following.	If the accounting period ending in year 2 is 12 or more months long, use the 12 months to that date. If the accounting period ending in year 2 is less than 12 months long, use the first 12 months of trading. If there is no accounting date in year 2, use the year itself (6/4 – 5/4).	12 months to accounting date in year 3.

Any profits taxed twice in the opening years are called overlap profits.

Overlap profits may be relieved on cessation.

Final year

Overlap profits are deducted from the final year's profits.

Assessment focus

You can easily check any computation that stretches over the whole life of a business. The total taxable profits (less losses) should equal the total actual profits (less actual losses).

Profits as adjusted for tax

Final year

The basis period for the final year starts at the end of the basis period for the previous year, and ends at cessation.

Example

Nitin, who has been trading for many years, prepares accounts to 30 June each year. Overlap profits of £9,000 arose when Nitin started trading. Results for recent years have been:

Y/e 30.6.19	£50,000
Y/e 30.6.20	£70,000

On 30.9.20 Nitin ceased trading. Profits for the three months to 30.9.20 were £15,000. What is Nitin's final trading profit assessment?

The trade ends in 2020/21 so 2020/21 is the final year

The basis period for 2019/20 would have been the y/e 30.6.19. The basis period for 2020/21 therefore runs from 1.7.19

Overlap profits are deducted from the final year's assessment

Solution

- 2020/21 is the final year of trade.
- The basis period is the period 1.7.19 – 30.9.20.
- The assessment for 2020/21 is:

	£
Y/e 30.6.20	70,000
3 m/e 30.9.20	15,000
Less: overlap profits	(9,000)
	76,000

Year of change = Tax year with new accounting date

Year before	Year of change	Year after
CYB to old accounting date	Tax the gap < 12m: Create new overlap from year before > 12m: Relieve overlap b/f	CYB to new accounting date

6: Partnerships

Topic List

Sharing profits between partners

A partnership's results are computed in the same way as the results of a sole trader. Once the results are found, they can then be allocated to individual partners.

1. Compute taxable trading profits for a partnership as a whole in the same way as you would compute the profits for a sole trader.
   - This means starting with the accounts profit and adding back disallowables/deducting amounts specifically deductible under the tax rules.
2. Divide results for each period of account between partners.
3. Tax each partner as if they were running their own business, and making profits and losses equal to their share of the firm's results for each period of account.
   - When a partner joins, the first period of account for their own business runs from the date of joining to the firm's next accounting date. The normal basis period rules for opening years apply.
   - When a partner leaves, the last period of account for their own business runs from the firm's most recent accounting date to the day they leave. The normal cessation rules apply.

Dividing results of each period of account between partners:

1 First, allocate salaries and interest on capital.

Remember to pro-rate the annual salary/interest if the period concerned is not 12 months long

2 Second, share the balance of the firm's results among the partners according to the profit-sharing arrangement for the period of account.

Example

Tim and Patrick are in partnership. They take annual salaries of £10,000 each, and thereafter share profits 60% to Tim and 40% to Patrick. Profits of £100,000 were made in the six months to 30 September 2020. Show what amount is allocated to each partner.

	Tim	Patrick	Total
	£	£	£
Salary (6/12)	5,000	5,000	10,000
Balance	54,000	36,000	90,000
	59,000	41,000	100,000

Notes

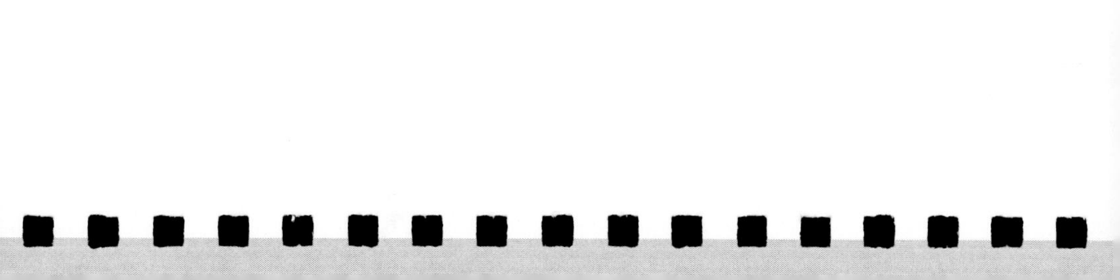

7: National Insurance

Topic List

In this chapter we look at NICs paid by the self-employed. These are the only NICs that are assessable.

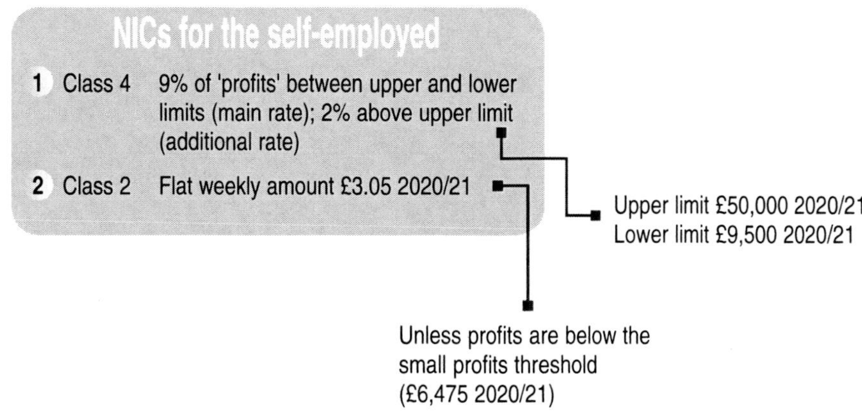
NICs for the self-employed
1 Class 4 9% of 'profits' between upper and lower limits (main rate); 2% above upper limit (additional rate)
2 Class 2 Flat weekly amount £3.05 2020/21
Upper limit £50,000 2020/21
Lower limit £9,500 2020/21
Unless profits are below the small profits threshold (£6,475 2020/21)

8: Losses

Topic List

Individuals: Carry forward of trading losses

Individuals: Deduction from total income

Companies: Trading losses

Companies: Other losses

In this chapter we will see how tax relief is obtained for trading losses, for all types of businesses.

There is no general rule that sole traders can get relief for their losses. The conditions of a specific relief must be complied with. We look at these reliefs in this chapter.

The methods of relieving losses for a company are different from the methods of relief for an individual. Do not confuse the two.

A Trading Loss in a basis period is calculated in exactly the same way as a taxable trading profit would be. The loss must then be allocated to the correct tax year. Eg a loss for y/e 31.12.20 would be allocated to 2020/21.

Carry forward

A loss not otherwise relieved is deducted from the first available profits of the same trade.

Losses **must** be deducted from the first available profits: they cannot be saved up until it suits the trader.

Losses may be carried forward for any number of years, but if the trade changes there is no further relief.

Relief

Loss is deducted from total income of the tax year of the loss and/or the preceding tax year.

Partial claims are not allowed; the whole loss must be deducted, so far as there is income available to absorb it in the chosen tax year of relief.

Loss can also be set against gains of the year of the loss and/or the preceding tax year.

Loss must be set against income of the relevant year first.

Assessment focus

Before recommending these reliefs, consider whether they would lead to the waste of the personal allowance or annual exempt amount. This is often a significant tax planning point.

Example

Sue makes up accounts to 30 September. Recent results are:

Y/e 30.9.20	£(50,000)
Y/e 30.9.21	£25,000

Results for the tax years are:

2020/21	£(50,000):	Loss
2021/22	£25,000:	Profit

Trading losses are the losses made by a company in its trade.

Trading losses

A company's trading loss may be:

(1) Set against other profits of the same accounting period.

- **Before** qualifying charitable donations. These may remain unrelieved.

(2) Set against profits of the previous 12 months.

- **Before** qualifying charitable donations. These may remain unrelieved.

(3) Carried forward to set against future taxable total profits.

- **Before** qualifying charitable donations. However the amount of the claim can be flexible so as not to waste the qualifying charitable donations.

Old rules

Trading losses generated before 1.4.17 could only be carried forward against future profits from the same trade. You are expected to be aware of this rule but will not be asked to do any calculations using it.

- A company can choose to claim relief (1) only
- If relief (2) is to be claimed, relief (1) must be claimed first

Tax planning

- Consider the timing of relief and the extent to which any qualifying charitable donations for companies (or personal allowance for an individual) become unrelieved

Capital losses

- Only set against current or future gains, never income
- Cannot be carried back

9: Self assessment for individuals

Topic List

Returns

Records

Payment of tax

Interest and late payment of tax

Compliance checks and enquiries

This chapter looks at when returns must be filed and at due dates for the payment of tax.

Filing date

The **filing due date** for filing a tax return online is:

(1) 31 January following the end of the tax year that the return covers; or

(2) 3 months after the notice to file a return was issued if issued after 31 October following the end of the tax year.

If an individual wishes to file a paper return, the filing date is 31 October following the tax year.

Penalties for late filing

The maximum penalties for delivering a return after the filing due date are:

(1) Initial penalty:	£100
(2) Return more than 3 months late:	£10 per day (max 90 days)
(3) Return more than 6 months but not more than 12 months late:	5% of tax due (min £300)
(4) Return more than 12 months late:	100% of tax due if deliberate and concealed 70% of tax due if deliberate but not concealed 5% of tax due, otherwise (min £300 each case) (eg careless)

Penalties for error

Imposed if inaccurate return for:

- Carelessness
- Deliberate error but no arrangements to conceal
- Deliberate error and arrangements to conceal

Amount of penalty

PLR is potential lost revenue eg tax unpaid

Reduced if error disclosed to HMRC

	Maximum of PLR	Minimum of PLR	
		Unprompted disclosure	Prompted disclosure
Careless	30%	0%	15%
Deliberate, not concealed	70%	20%	35%
Deliberate, concealed	100%	30%	50%

Records

Records must, in general, be kept until the later of:

(1) Five years after the 31 January following the tax year concerned (where the taxpayer is in business or has rental income); or

(2) One year after the 31 January following the tax year, otherwise.

Failure to keep records could lead to a penalty of £3,000 for each tax year concerned.

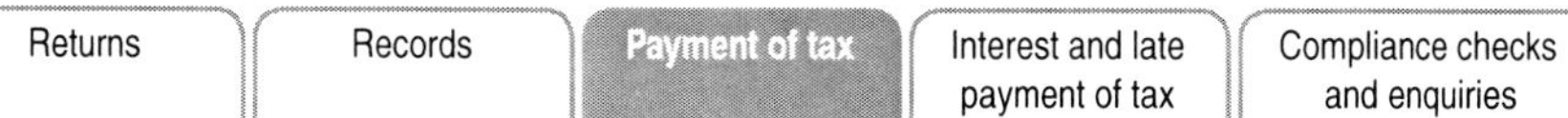

Payment of tax

Payments on account (POA) must be made on 31 January in tax year and on the following 31 July.

The final payment of income tax must be paid on 31 January following the tax year.

Payments on account

1. Each POA is 50% of the prior tax year's liability less tax suffered at source.
2. POAs are not required if the prior year's income tax payable falls below £1,000 or more than 80% of prior year liability met at source.
3. A claim may be made to reduce POAs to a stated amount, or nil.

Late payment of tax

Penalties are levied on late payment of a final payment of income tax, Class 4 NICs or CGT as follows:

Paid	Penalty
Not more than 5 months after penalty date	5% of unpaid tax
More than 5 months but not more than 11 months after penalty date	10% of unpaid tax
More than 11 months after penalty date	15% of unpaid tax

Penalty date is 30 days after the due date for tax

Interest

Interest runs on:

(1) POAs from the normal due dates (31 Jan and 31 July)

(2) Any final payment, and CGT, from the due date (31 January following tax year)

Compliance checks

- Pre-return checks using information powers
- Enquiries into returns/claims/elections already submitted

Enquiries

HMRC may enquire into a return provided they give notice by a year after the receipt of the return (if the return is filed on or before the filing due date).

If return filed late: a year from the next 31 January, 30 April, 31 July, 31 October after actual filing date

HMRC randomly select returns to compliance check. They also select returns where there is an identified tax risk.

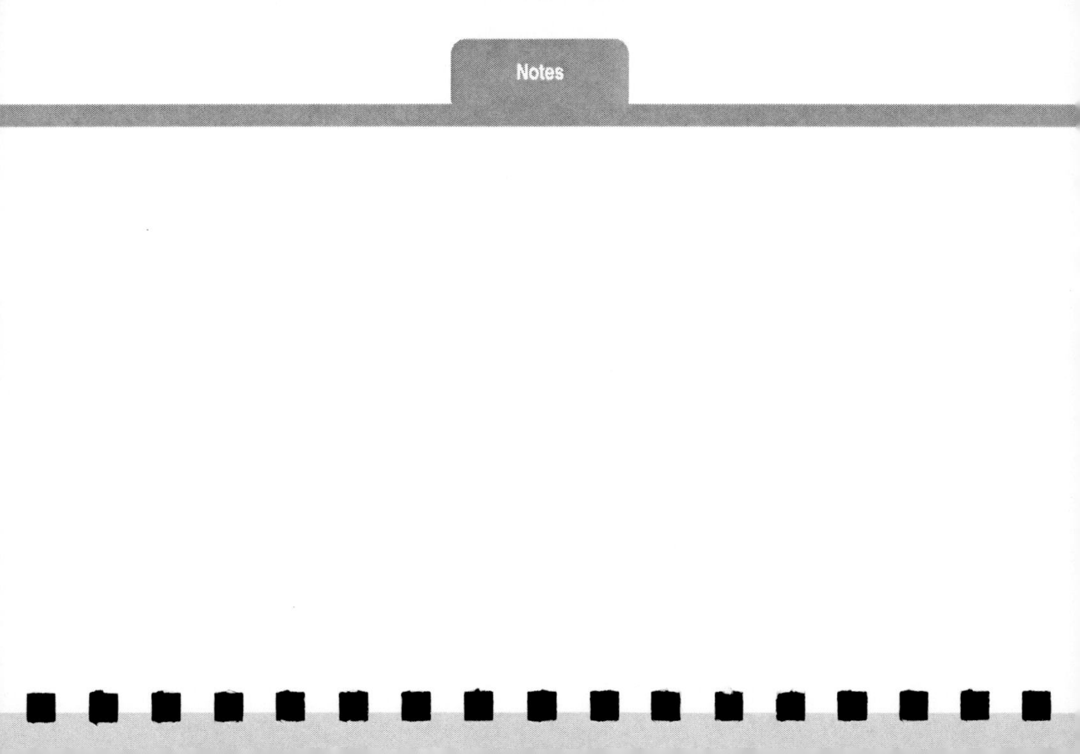

Notes

10: Self assessment for companies

Topic List

In this chapter we look at both the administration of corporation tax (CT) and at when that tax must be paid. As the due dates for payment of CT impact on a company's cash flow position, it is vitally important to be aware of these dates.

Returns

A company must normally file its CT return by the filing due date which is the later of:

- 12 months after the end of the period of account
- 3 months after a notice requiring the return was issued

Enquiries

Notice to enquire into a return must be given by 12 months after the later of:

- The actual filing date (if filed on or before filing due date); or
- The 31 January, 30 April, 31 July or 31 October next following the actual filing date (if filed after filing due date)

Companies must file **online**

Late filing of return – as for individuals

Penalties for error – as for individuals

Records must generally be kept for six years from the end of the accounting period concerned.

Due dates

- 'Large' companies must pay their CT in instalments.
- Other companies must pay their CT nine months and one day after the end of the accounting period (AP).

A company with augmented profits above the upper limit of £1,500,000

Augmented profits are taxable total profits plus dividends received from UK companies

Ignore dividends from related 51% group companies

Quarterly instalments

- For a 12 month AP instalments are due in:
  - Months 7 and 10 of the period
  - Months 1 and 4 of the following period
- Instalments due on 14th day of month concerned

Interest runs from the due date. Interest paid is a tax deductible expense for companies.

Upper limit

The upper limit is:

- Multiplied by months/12 for short accounting periods
- Divided by the number of related 51% group companies in the group

Companies under the control of the same parent company

Example

A Ltd, which has one related 51% group company, prepares accounts for the nine months to 31.3.21. The upper limit for this period is:

$$9/12 \times \frac{£1,500,000}{2} = £562,500$$

Small/medium-sized enterprise

- Less than 500 employees

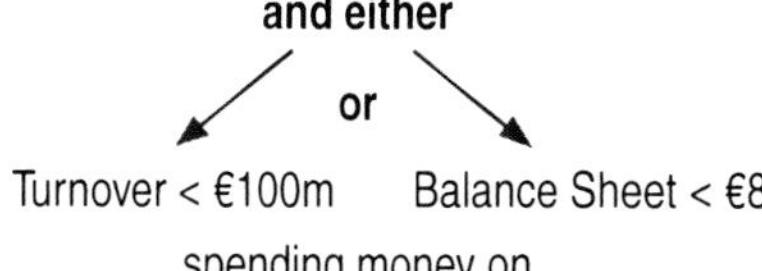

spending money on

Research & Development → **230% relief**

- R&D staff
- Consumables/transformable materials
- Computer software
- Power, water, fuel

- If relief creates/increases a loss surrender loss for R&D tax credit @ 14.5% (capped at PAYE/NIC liability)

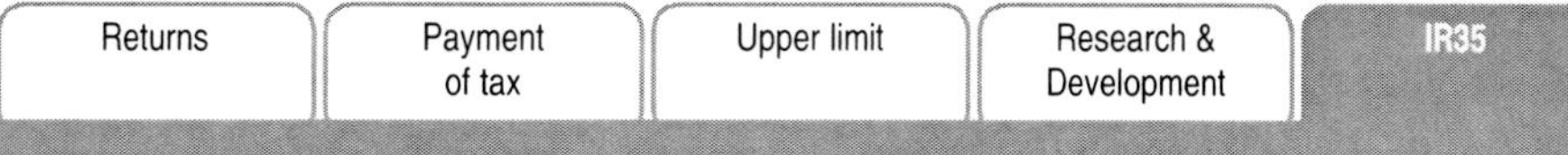

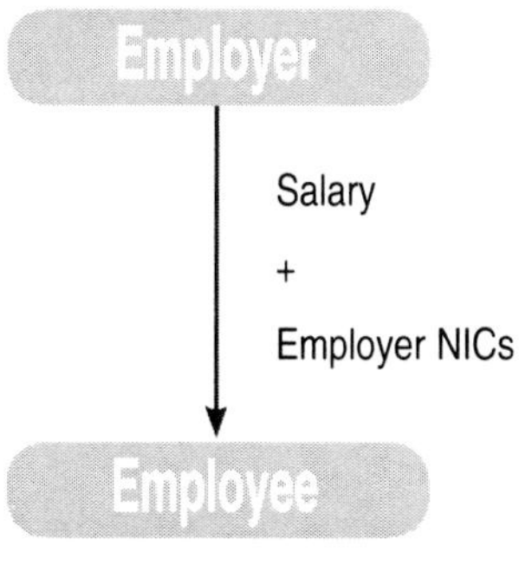

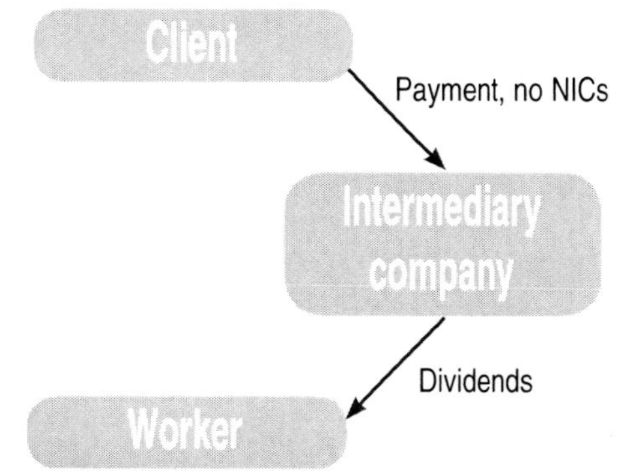

If the relationship between client and worker is really one of employment, then IR35 applies. Worker is taxed on deemed employment income.

11: Chargeable gains – the basics

Topic List

- Chargeable persons, disposals and assets
- Basic computation for individuals
- The charge to CGT for individuals
- Losses for individuals
- Computing gains and losses for a company

It is important that you can calculate chargeable gains realised by both sole traders and companies. The computations are similar but not identical.

Chargeable persons, disposals and assets

Three elements are needed for a chargeable gain to arise:

1. A **chargeable disposal**: this includes sales, gifts and the destruction of assets.
2. A **chargeable person**: companies and individuals.
3. A **chargeable asset**: most assets are chargeable; exempt assets include cars and some chattels (eg racehorses).

Computation

Compute a gain as follows:

	£
Proceeds	X
Less: cost	(X)
Chargeable gain	X

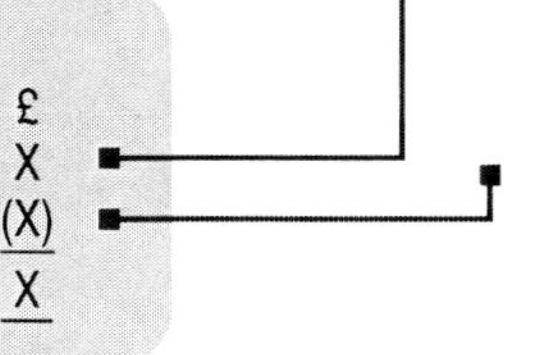

- **Actual proceeds** or **market value** in the case of gifts and disposals that are not bargains at arm's length, after costs of disposal.

- Include:

  (1) **Original cost** of the asset or **market value** if that was used as proceeds for the person who sold the asset to the individual.

  (2) **Enhancement expenditure** reflected in the state and nature of the asset at the time of disposal.

  (3) **Incidental costs** of **acquisition**.

Deduct the CGT annual exempt amount of £12,300 (2020/21) when computing an individual's total taxable gains.

Rate

- 20% if higher or additional rate taxpayer
- 10% on taxable gains up to the amount of the unused basic rate band and 20% on the excess

Due date

CGT for 2020/21 is due on 31 January 2022

Example

Sue made taxable gains (after the annual exempt amount) in July 2020 of £10,000.

She has £6,000 of unused basic rate band.

What CGT must Sue pay?

She must pay CGT of
£6,000 × 10% + £4,000 × 20%
= £1,400

Deduct allowable capital losses from chargeable gains in the tax year in which they arise.

Any loss that cannot be set off is carried forward to set against future chargeable gains.

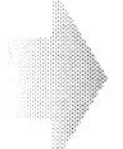

Allowable losses brought forward are offset against gains after the annual exempt amount

Example

Zoë made gains of £19,000 in 2020/21. She had brought forward capital losses of £8,000.

The gain after the annual exempt amount is £6,700, so £6,700 of the brought-forward losses are offset in 2020/21 after the annual exempt amount has been deducted. The remaining £1,300 will be carried forward to 2021/22.

Computation

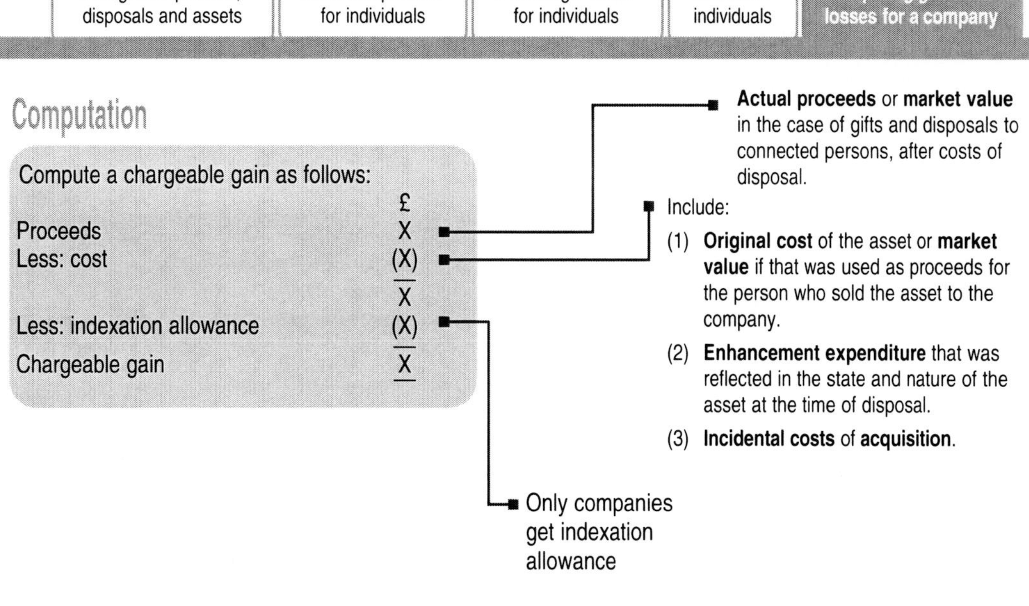

Compute a chargeable gain as follows:

	£
Proceeds	X
Less: cost	(X)
	X
Less: indexation allowance	(X)
Chargeable gain	X

- **Actual proceeds** or **market value** in the case of gifts and disposals to connected persons, after costs of disposal.
- Include:
  (1) **Original cost** of the asset or **market value** if that was used as proceeds for the person who sold the asset to the company.
  (2) **Enhancement expenditure** that was reflected in the state and nature of the asset at the time of disposal.
  (3) **Incidental costs** of **acquisition**.
- Only companies get indexation allowance

Indexation allowance

- Expenditure multiplied by indexation factor
- Runs from date of acquisition to December 2017 or date of disposal if earlier
- Index expenditure incurred on different dates separately eg enhancement expenditure
- Does not apply to disposal costs

Indexation factor

Will be given to you in assessment

Losses

Indexation allowance cannot create or increase an allowable loss

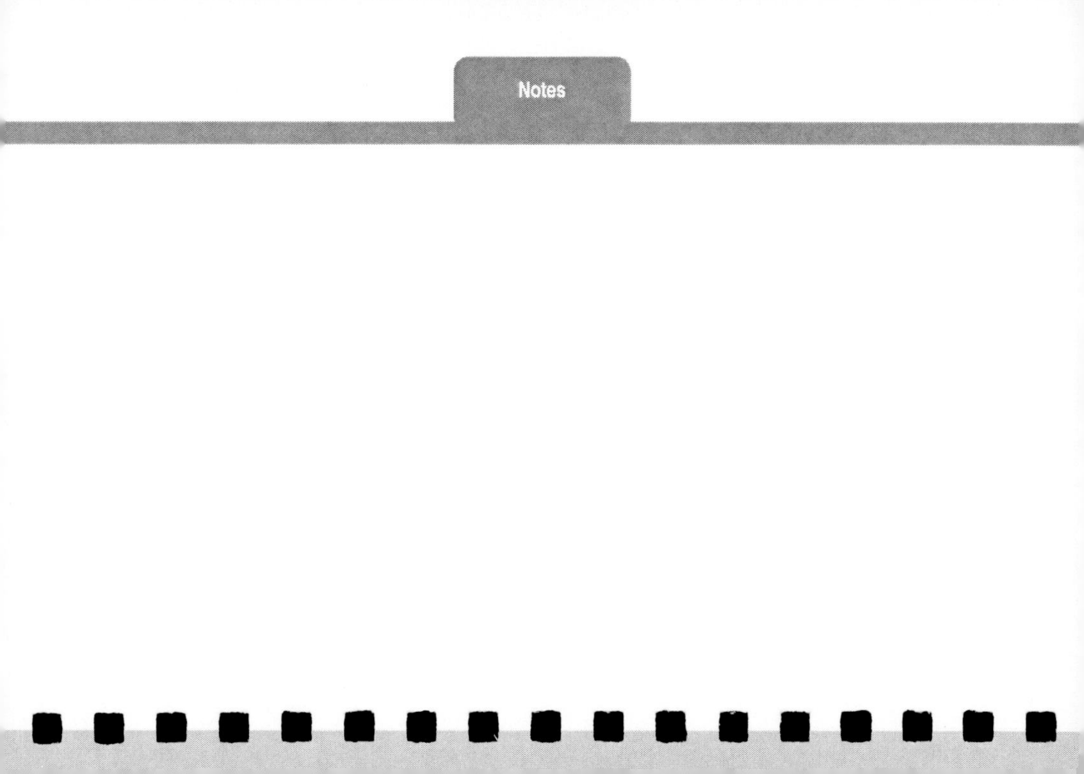
Notes

12: Further aspects of chargeable gains

Topic List

Part disposals

Chattels

Connected persons

Spouses and civil partners

In this chapter we look at some specific rules applying to part disposals and chattels for both companies and individuals.

We finish the chapter on rules that relate to individuals only, when disposals are made to connected persons, or spouses/civil partners.

Part disposals

On a part disposal, you are only allowed to take part of the cost of the asset into account.

- Costs attributable solely to the part disposed of are taken into account in full
- For other costs, take into account A/(A+B) of the cost
  - A is the proceeds of the part sold
  - B is the market value of the part retained

Example

Peter owns land that originally cost £30,000. He sold a quarter interest in the land for £18,000. The incidental costs of disposal were £1,000. The market value of the three-quarter share remaining is estimated to be £36,000. What is the chargeable gain?

	£
Proceeds	18,000
Less: incidental costs of disposal	(1,000)
Less: $\frac{18,000}{18,000+36,000} \times 30,000$	(10,000)
Chargeable gain	7,000

Chattels

A chattel is an item of **tangible moveable property** (eg a painting).

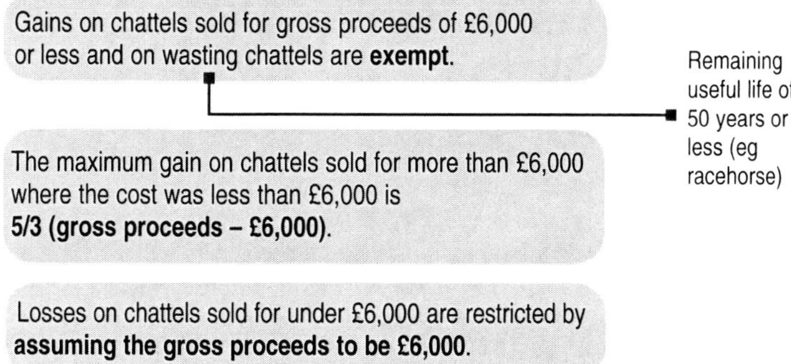

Disposals between connected persons are deemed to be for the **market values** of the assets. If a loss arises on a disposal to a connected person it can only be set against chargeable gains on disposals to the **same** connected person.

An individual is connected with his relatives, his spouse/civil partner's relatives (brothers, sisters, ancestors and lineal descendants) and their spouses/civil partners.

Exception: does not apply to 'no gain/no loss' disposals (see spouses and civil partners)

Spouses and civil partners

Disposals between spouses/civil partners do not give rise to gains or losses.

The spouse/civil partner acquiring the asset is deemed to buy it for proceeds resulting in neither a gain nor a loss.

Effect is that acquiring spouse/civil partner takes asset at base cost of disposing spouse/civil partner.

Example

Joe buys an asset for £20,000 and gives it to his wife Julie when its market value is £30,000.

	£
Deemed proceeds	20,000
Less: cost	(20,000)
	No gain/no loss

Julie's base cost for future disposals is £20,000.

Notes

13: Share disposals

Topic List

Matching rules for individuals

Bonus and rights issues for individuals

Matching rules for companies

FA 1985 pool

Bonus and rights issues for companies

The special rules for shares disposed of by both individuals and companies are covered in this chapter.

Shares of one class in one company are all identical, but they may have been bought at different times, for different prices. We therefore need matching rules to work out which shares have been sold, so that we can identify the cost of shares sold.

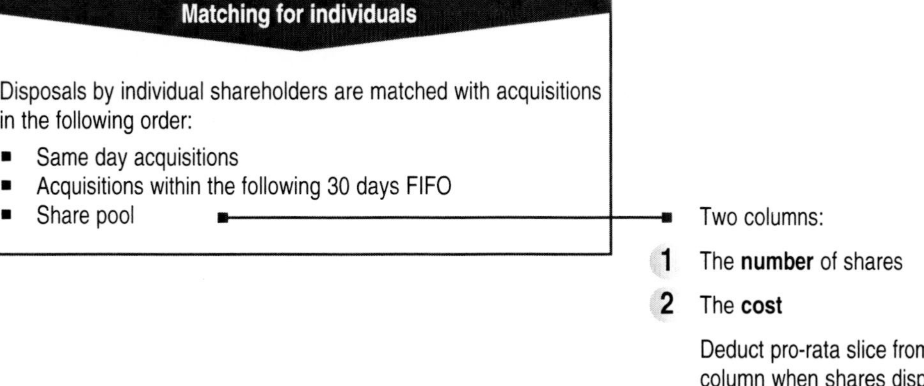

Matching for individuals

Disposals by individual shareholders are matched with acquisitions in the following order:

- Same day acquisitions
- Acquisitions within the following 30 days FIFO
- Share pool

Two columns:

1. The **number** of shares
2. The **cost**

Deduct pro-rata slice from cost column when shares disposed of.

Bonus issues

Simply add the number of shares to share pool; there is no cost

Rights issues

Add number of shares and cost to share pool

The matching rules for shares held by a company are different from the matching rules for shares held by an individual. Take care not to confuse the two.

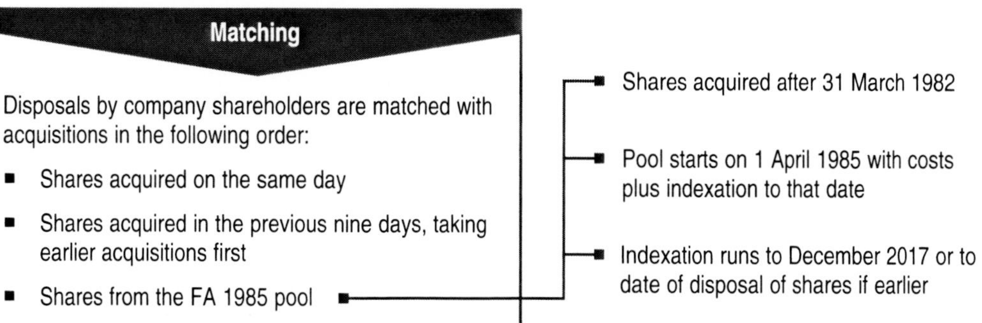

Matching

Disposals by company shareholders are matched with acquisitions in the following order:

- Shares acquired on the same day
- Shares acquired in the previous nine days, taking earlier acquisitions first
- Shares from the FA 1985 pool
  - Shares acquired after 31 March 1982
  - Pool starts on 1 April 1985 with costs plus indexation to that date
  - Indexation runs to December 2017 or to date of disposal of shares if earlier

Where shares are disposed of within nine days of acquisition, no indexation allowance is available even if the acquisition and the disposal fall in different months. Acquisitions matched with disposals under the nine day rule never enter the FA 1985 pool.

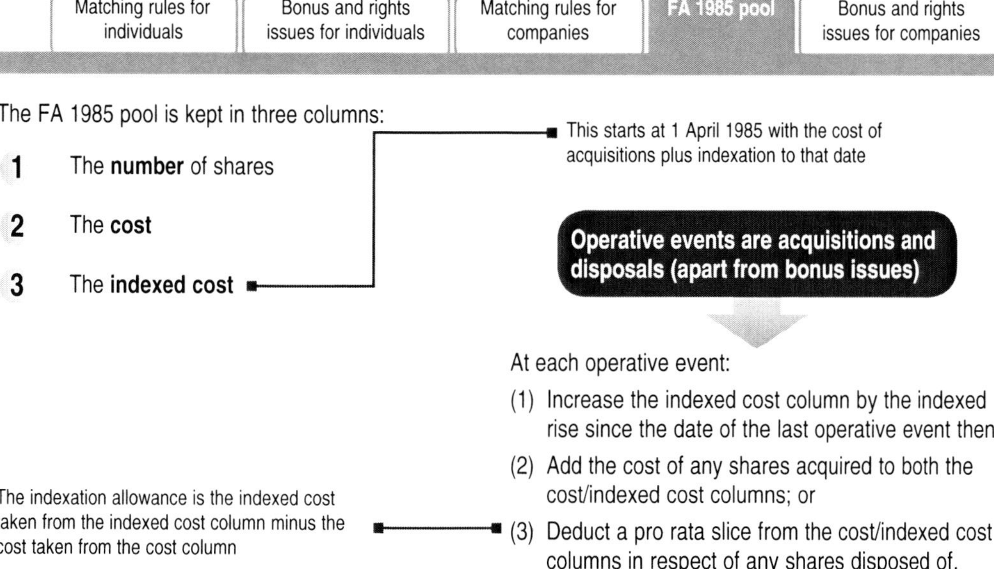

The FA 1985 pool is kept in three columns:

1. The **number** of shares
2. The **cost**
3. The **indexed cost**

This starts at 1 April 1985 with the cost of acquisitions plus indexation to that date

Operative events are acquisitions and disposals (apart from bonus issues)

At each operative event:

(1) Increase the indexed cost column by the indexed rise since the date of the last operative event then

(2) Add the cost of any shares acquired to both the cost/indexed cost columns; or

(3) Deduct a pro rata slice from the cost/indexed cost columns in respect of any shares disposed of.

The indexation allowance is the indexed cost taken from the indexed cost column minus the cost taken from the cost column

Bonus issues

- Bonus issues relating to the FA 1985 pool go into that pool
- Simply add the number of shares to FA 1985 pool; there is no cost

Rights issues

Rights issues relating to FA 1985 pool shares are treated as an operative event. Index the pool to the date of the rights issue if prior to December 2017, and then add in the cost and number of rights issue shares. If the rights issue occurs post December 2017 there will be no further indexation so simply add in the number and cost of the rights shares.

14: Reliefs for chargeable gains

Topic List

- Investors' relief
- Business asset disposal relief
- Rollover relief
- Gift relief

In the assessment you should look out for the availability of various reliefs. However, do take care to ensure that you do not claim relief when you are not allowed to.

Business asset disposal relief reduces the rate of CGT payable on certain business assets to 10%, regardless of the level of income.

Rollover relief applies for individuals and companies when certain assets used in a business are sold and other business assets purchased.

Gift relief is available on certain types of assets. You must be able to identify the assets that qualify for gift relief and discuss how the relief operates.

Investors' relief reduces the rate of CGT payable on disposal of certain shares to 10%.

Conditions

- Subscribe for shares which are issued on or after 17 March 2016
- The shares are ordinary shares in an unlisted, trading company
- The individual has not been an employee or officer of the company during the ownership period.
- The shares are held continuously for three years from the date of issue or from 6 April 2016 where the shares are issued between 17 March and 5 April 2016,

Gain are taxed at 10% up to a life time limit of £10,000,000

Claims

By first anniversary of 31 January following end of tax year of disposal

Investors' relief | **Business asset disposal relief** | Rollover relief | Gift relief

Conditions

Material disposal of business assets:

- Disposal of whole or part of business owned for at least two years
- Disposal of assets used for business on cessation if business owned for at least two years and disposal within three years of cessation
- Disposal of trading company shares where company is personal company and individual is officer or employee, all for at least two years

Claims

By first anniversary of 31 January following end of tax year of disposal

- Personal company: individual holds at least 5% of ordinary shares and voting rights

How it works

- Qualifying gains taxed at 10%, regardless of the level of income
- Lifetime limit of £1 million eligible gains (£10 million prior to 11 March 2020)
- Gains eligible for business asset disposal relief are treated as the lowest slice of gains

Example

Chris sells his business in November 2020. The gains are £150,000. He also has another non business gain of £17,400 for 2020/21. Chris has taxable income of £30,000 for 2020/21. What is his CGT payable?

	£
Gains qualifying for business asset disposal relief	
£150,000 × 10%	15,000
Other gains	
(£17,400 – £12,300) × 20%	1,020
	16,020

Uses up remaining basic rate band first

Taxpayers can claim to defer gains arising on the disposal of business assets that are being replaced if both the old and the new assets are on the list of eligible assets and are used in the trade.

The new asset must be bought in the period starting 12 months before and ending 36 months after the disposal.

If rollover relief is claimed the deferred gain is deducted from the base cost of the new asset.

Eligible assets

- Land and buildings used for the purposes of the trade
- Fixed (that is, immoveable) plant and machinery
- Goodwill (for individuals only)

If disposal proceeds are only partially reinvested in the new asset, an amount of the gain equal to the proceeds not reinvested is immediately chargeable. The remainder of the gain can be deferred.

Example

Prianka sold land used in her business for £500,000 realising a gain of £150,000. Two months later she bought an office building for £480,000.

An amount of the gain equal to the proceeds not reinvested in the office, £20,000, is immediately chargeable. The remaining gain, £130,000 may be rolled over. The rolled over gain is deducted from the base cost of the building, which will then become £350,000 (£480,000 – £130,000).

When gift relief is **claimed**, the gain on the gift is deducted from the recipient's base cost.

Qualifying assets

- Business assets qualifying for gift relief are:
  - Assets used in a trade carried on by donor/donor's personal company
  - Shares and securities in either an unquoted trading company or in the donor's personal trading company

Individual holds at least 5% voting rights

Notes

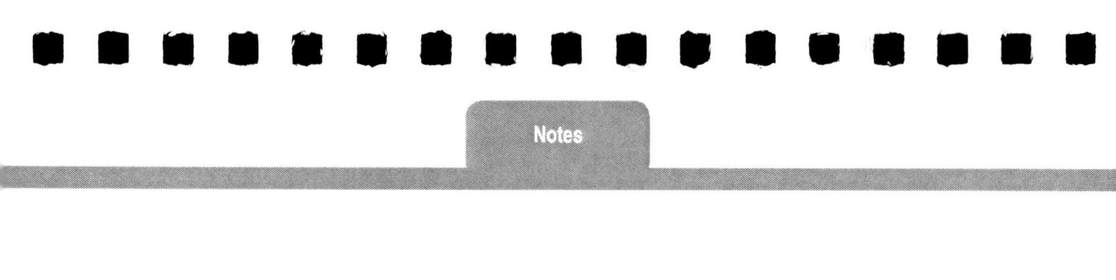

Notes

Notes

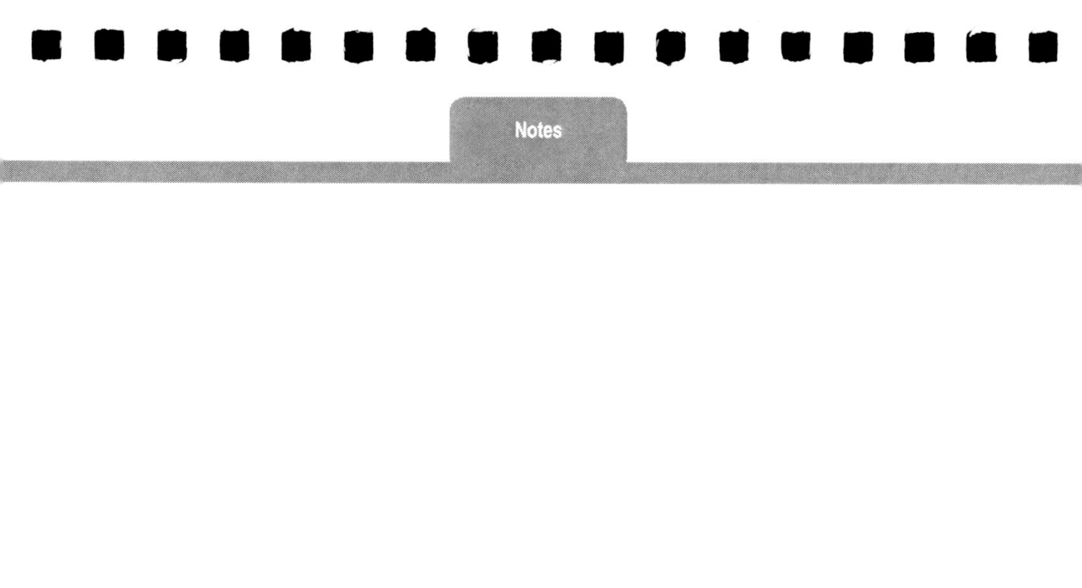

Notes

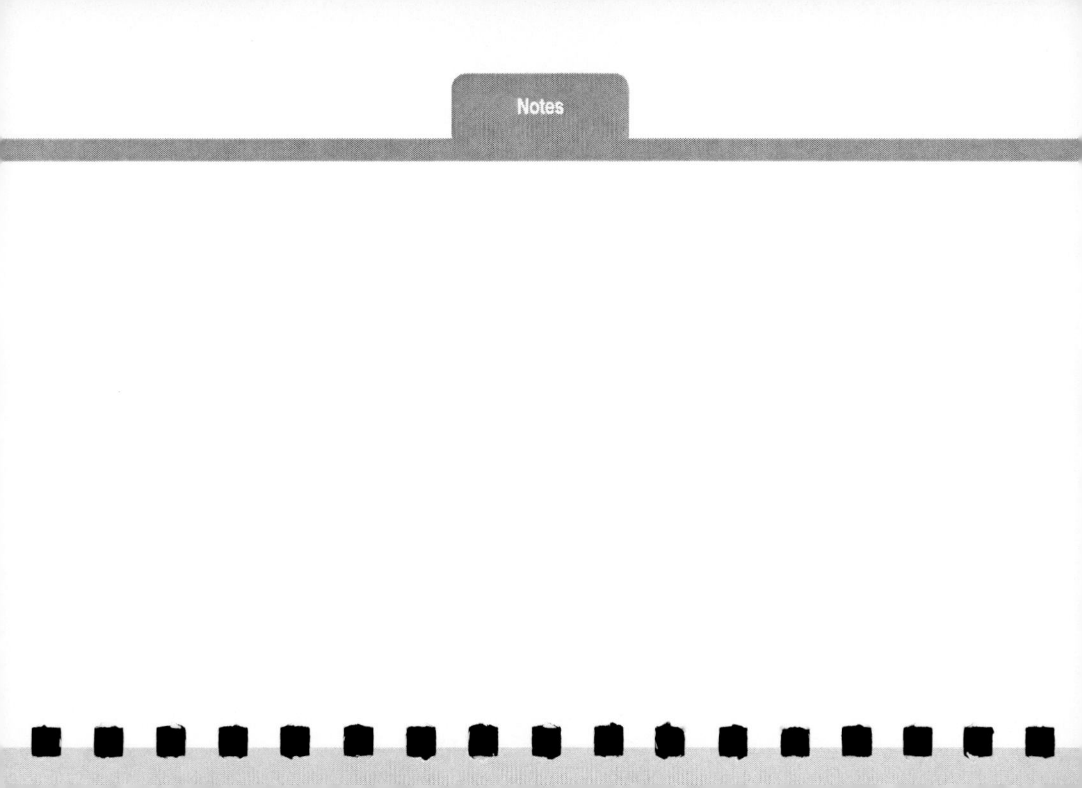

Notes

Notes

Notes